THE ODD ONE OUT
ANIMALS!

© 2017 Webber Books

All rights reserved. This book or any portion thereof may not be reproduced or used in any manner whatsoever without the express written permission of the publisher except for the use of brief quotations in a book review.

Images by freepix, terdpongvector

iN THE FOREST!
WHO'S THE ODD ONE OUT?

THE ODD ONE OUT is.....

THE SHEEP!

SOMETHING FISHY!
WHO'S THE ODD ONE OUT?

THE ODD ONE OUT is.....

THE TORTOISE!

ON THE FARM!
WHO'S THE ODD ONE OUT?

THE ODD ONE OUT is.....
THE SEAL!

CATS, CATS, CATS!
WHO'S THE ODD ONE OUT?

THE ODD ONE OUT is.....

THE DOG!

WILD ANIMALS!
WHO'S THE ODD ONE OUT?

THE ODD ONE OUT IS.....
THE COW!

ANIMALS WEARING GLASSES!
WHO'S THE ODD ONE OUT?

THE ODD ONE OUT iS.....

THiS ONE !

iNSECTS AND BUGS!
WHO'S THE ODD ONE OUT?

THE ODD ONE OUT IS.....

THE TOUCAN BiRD!

ALL THINGS ARCTIC!
WHO'S THE ODD ONE OUT?

THE ODD ONE OUT is.....

THE KOALA BEAR!

FRUITY FRIENDS!
WHO'S THE ODD ONE OUT?

THE ODD ONE OUT IS.....

THE HEDGEHOG!

BIRDIE BIRD BIRDS!
WHO'S THE ODD ONE OUT?

THE ODD ONE OUT iS.....

THE BAT!

SEA CREATURES!
WHO'S THE ODD ONE OUT?

THE ODD ONE OUT iS.....

THE HORSE!

SCARVES AND HATS!
WHO'S THE ODD ONE OUT?

THE ODD ONE OUT iS.....

THE RABBiT!

BABY ANIMALS!
WHO'S THE ODD ONE OUT?

THE ODD ONE OUT iS....
THE ZEBRA!

NOT PETS!
WHO'S THE ODD ONE OUT?

THE ODD ONE OUT IS.....

THE DOG!

FOUR-LEGGED FRIENDS!

WHO'S THE ODD ONE OUT?

THE ODD ONE OUT iS.....

THE OSTRiCH!

WE CAN FLY!
WHO'S THE ODD ONE OUT?

THE ODD ONE OUT is.....

THE CHICKEN!

SPEEDY ANIMALS!
WHO'S THE ODD ONE OUT?

THE ODD ONE OUT iS.....
THE SNAIL!

WE'VE GOT TAILS!
WHO'S THE ODD ONE OUT?

THE ODD ONE OUT IS...

THE JELLYFISH!

THE END!

19927108R00025

Printed in Poland
by Amazon Fulfillment
Poland Sp. z o.o., Wrocław